FUN WITH SCIENCE

TREES AND LEAVES

ROSIE HARLOW & GARETH MORGAN

Contents

Use the symbols below to help you identify the three kinds of practical activities in this book.

EXPERIMENTS

TRICKS

THINGS TO MAKE

WARWICK PRESS

Introduction

Trees are the largest living things in the world. Some, such as the giant redwood can reach heights of 360 feet. Though tall, they are not the biggest trees. That record goes to a particular Californian sequoia which is 270 feet high and 79 feet around the trunk. If uprooted it would weigh 2,145 tons. Though to us trees seem like giants they are closely related to small garden plants which we dwarf. Like all plants, trees can convert sunlight into food. In doing so they change carbon dioxide from the atmosphere into sugars for their growth and release oxygen which animals breathe. For this reason the great rain forests, where millions of trees are found, have been called the "lungs of the planet."

Five thousand years ago nearly three-fourths of the world's land area was covered by trees. Today between 70 and 90 percent of these have been cut down and huge areas are cut down every minute. An area of trees acts as an air purifier, a power station, and a housing complex. Clearing these areas makes people homeless, kills the animals living there, and ultimately affects our ability to survive.

This book covers seven main topics:
- What a tree is made of
- How a tree grows
- Leaves and why they fall
- How trees reproduce
- The animals that live in trees
- How wood is used
- Saving the great forests

A blue line (like the one around the edge of these two pages) indicates the start of a new topic.

►How can you find out how old or high a tree is? (page 5)

▼How many different types of leaf are there and how do they work? (pages 14–21)

▼Where do trees come from and how do they reproduce? (page 22)

▲How does a twig tell its own history and what is inside a bud? (page 13)

▲How do trees grow and why can squirrels damage them so easily? (page 11)

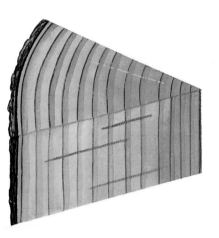

▲How do trees grow? (page 10)

▼How can you preserve leaves to keep as a record? (page 18)

▲Why does a tree have leaves and why do they change color and fall? (page 20)

▼Where do fruits and seeds come from and why are they important? (page 26)

3

What Is a Tree?

Plants are different from other living things because they can use sunlight to make food and grow. To reach the light, plants have evolved tall thin stems. Trees are different from other plants because they have a tough woody stem. Look at the trees growing in gardens, parks, and woods near you. They are very exciting when you find out how they work.

Where Does Your Tree Live?

This tree is called "Crinkle Leaf." Its address is 50 Paces From the Back Door, Near the Shed, Back Yard.

Be a Tree Agent

Choose a tree that is in a garden, park, field, or wood near you. We shall now try to help you discover how your tree is special and why it is important. Just as agents advertise for sale houses for people to live in, so you can be a tree agent by making a poster to advertise your tree and encourage creatures to come and live there. (For trees are homes for many, many creatures.)

Tree Fingers

You need a small mirror. Stand at the edge of your tree and hold the mirror flat with one end on your nose. Look down into the mirror. You should be able to see the twigs of your tree. The little twigs are like the tree's "fingers" stretching into the sky. Follow one finger in toward its arm (branch) and then to its shoulder (where it joins the trunk).

Tree Skeletons

Stand about 30 paces from your tree and draw it. But first look very carefully at it. Notice how each branch splits and divides from the trunk to the finger tips.

How Old Is Your Tree?

Use a piece of string (or tape measure) to measure the **girth** (the distance around the middle) of your tree. It is most accurate if you measure it at about 3 feet high.

Every inch around the girth corresponds to about one year in a tree's growth.

Measure at 3 feet high

Work out the area covered by the branches of your trees. Walk from the trunk to the edge of the crown in eight different directions. Draw this using half an inch for one pace. Join these so you can see the shape of the crown. Use your diagram to work out the area of the crown.

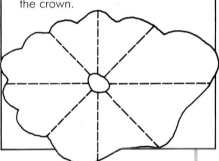

How High Is Your Tree?

Stand about 15 paces from your tree. Hold a pencil at arm's length and line up the bottom of the pencil with the base of the tree. Gradually walk backward away from the tree until the tip of the pencil is lined up with the top of the tree. Turn the pencil so it is parallel to the ground, keeping it aligned with the base of the tree. The point on the ground that lines up with the end of the pencil is the place the top of the tree would land if it fell over. Pace out this distance to find out how tall the tree is.

Pencil

Match the tip of the pencil with the top of the tree and the base of the pencil with the base of the tree.

5

Make a Tree Poster

Make a tree poster like the one shown here, and use it to record what you find out about your tree.

Tree name Crinkle Leaf

Address 50 Paces from the Back Door, Near the Shed, Back Yard.

Age The foundations of this tree were built over 60 years ago and it has been growing ever since.

Roots Six sturdy feet (roots) provide firm foundations.

Bark Makes good thick walls to protect the inside of the tree. Tiny slits (lenticels) in the bark provide an air-conditioning system, letting air in and out.

Branches provide attractive old style timber structure for the upper stories making light, airy rooms available at all levels.

Twigs make stairs for smaller residents to climb to upper stories. Buds make upward extensions of the home, providing new rooms each year.

Buds and new leaves provide a constant supply of free meals for some residents (minibeasts, birds) and visitors (deer).

Leaves These are furnished rooms with meals provided for smaller tenants such as leaf miners.

Crown This tree has 270 square feet of crown area. This offers spacious rooftop balconies and gardens with excellent views.

Flowers and seeds Flowers from some trees (apple, horse chestnut) provide meals for visiting bees and butterflies. Seeds from our tree (acorns) provide food for squirrels.

Environmentally friendly This tree is environmentally friendly. Leaves produce oxygen. They also reduce the amount of carbon dioxide in the air.

Bonus Our tree has its own sound system. Sounds vary from the gentle sounds of the wind to the noisy music of birds chattering.

Further bonus Free decoration four times a year. Every season the tree home is redecorated. Summer colors, dark green, fall colors, browns, red, and orange, winter, black and white, spring, bright green.

In the shade Dead branches are outbuildings providing further accommodation for minibeasts.

Tree Music

Sit under your tree with your eyes closed. With your hand in a fist raise one finger each time you hear a new sound. Record the sounds you hear on a cardboard "tape" like these. Begin with your pencil on start. Go up if the noise gets louder or higher, go down if it gets softer or lower.

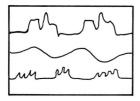

We recorded three sounds. The sound of a bird (*top*); the sound of the wind in the trees (*middle*); the sound of rustling and crunches in the leaves (*bottom*).

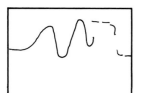

Choose one bird and try to record its song. This song rose and fell twice, followed by three high short notes and two low short notes.

Tree Scents

Every leaf has its own special scent. To discover the scent, crush the leaf between your fingers until the green juice comes out. Mix the crushed leaves in a half cup of water to make a cocktail. **Remember** some leaves such as privet can be poisonous!

Crushed leaves

Shake Hands with a Tree

When people meet they often shake hands. To meet a tree you need a blindfold. Tie a scarf around a friend's head carefully, so the person cannot see. Now lead your friend to any tree. He or she must get to know every detail of the tree by feeling it. Can they reach around its girth or waist? Help them feel for lumps and bumps and special touches and textures. When your friend has found out everything about the tree take off the blindfold. Can your friend find the same tree again by feeling and using his or her eyes as well? Swap over. Get to know your own tree with a blindfold on and mark all the bumps and cracks and crevices on your poster.

Warning Be careful to guide your friend carefully so they don't trip.

Make a Tree

Roll up three sheets of newspaper into a tube about an inch wide. Tape loosely. Cut down the tube as shown with wiggly or straight lines about half an inch apart. Pull up at point (A) from the inside sheet of paper. Paint the newspaper first with thin watercolors to make colored trees.

Equipment: Large newspaper, scissors, water color paints, tape, cardboard.

Cut tubes here to make leaves

Make a Forest

Cut a piece of thick cardboard from a box, paint it and lay it flat. Make many trees of different heights and colors. To stand your trees up, cut a finger of cardboard out from the base. Place the trunk over the finger and tape it down.

Cut tubes here to make roots

Tape roots to board

9

How Does a Tree Grow?

Trees grow in two ways. Outward growth occurs in the cambium layer. Each year, cells in this layer divide and grow. They grow outward pushing the bark, which eventually splits and falls off and is replaced. A tree's upward growth occurs at the tip of each twig.

Tree Transportation

The inward growth of the cambium forms the main part of the trunk. This is called xylem. Much of this wood is made up of dead or dying material but it still has a very important role to play. The xylem is made of tiny tubes which transport water and minerals from the roots up the trunk and branches to the leaves. Leaves need this water to help them make food from sunlight. The outward growth is provided by a layer of phloem. This is made up of tiny tubes that transport the sugars from the leaves to the rest of the tree. The phloem is very important and if it is damaged the tree will die.

Branch Scar

If a branch dies, it falls off and leaves a round-shaped scar. Look for branch scars on your tree.

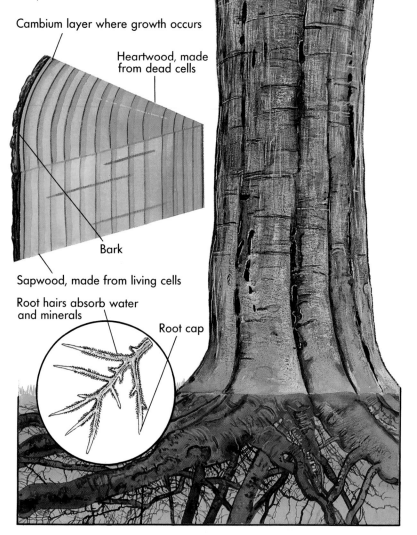

Cambium layer where growth occurs

Heartwood, made from dead cells

Bark

Sapwood, made from living cells

Root hairs absorb water and minerals

Root cap

Root Hairs

Roots may not go down deep but they can spread outward as far as the tree is tall. They have many tiny **root hairs.** These take essential moisture and minerals up into the tree. Root hairs increase the surface area of the root and increase the amount of water the tree can take up.

Proving Bark Is Important

Squirrels often eat bark, especially from tender young trees and twigs. They eat the bark in a ring around the twig or trunk. This destroys the important **cambium layer**, and the tree dies. Peel off half an inch of bark at the base of a small twig, as a squirrel might do to a young tree. Record what happens over the next few weeks.

Looking for Lenticels

Take a small new twig from your tree. Peel the top layer of bark off. Look for holes in it. These are partly filled with a powdery substance. This is loose cork from a cork layer under the bark. In summer these holes allow water out and air in. In winter they are sealed. As bark grows, the holes or **lenticels** stretch and split sideways.

Squirrels chew bark off twigs

Cut bark here

Lenticels

Weaving with Bark

Score some twigs at 4-inch intervals and all down one side (see below). Peel off the bark and flatten it between layers of newspaper for a few hours. Cut strips about ¼ inch wide. Lay four strips out to start. Weave four others in the opposite direction then gradually weave in more strips until your mat is finished.

Score along these lines

Bark Rubbing

All trees have a different bark pattern rather as people have fingerprints. Record different trees' "fingerprints" using wax crayons. Is bark the same all over the tree? Do rubbings at different heights to find out. Use some to illustrate your poster.

Tie paper around trunk

Rub with crayon

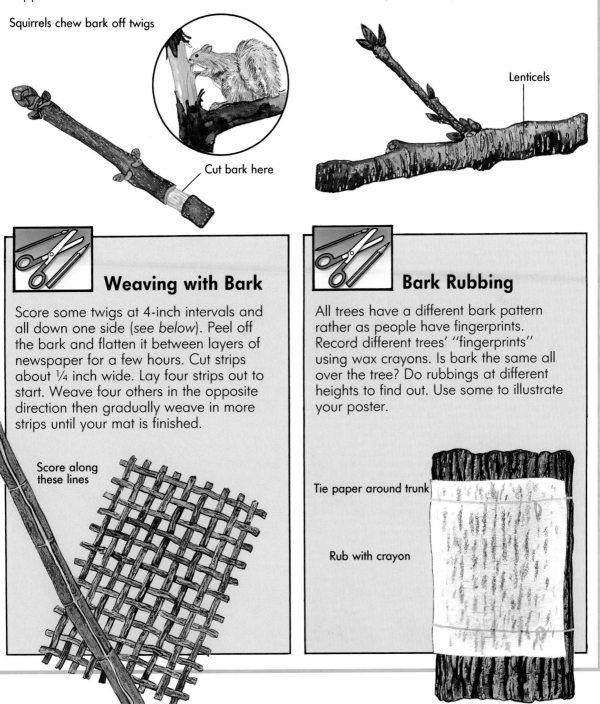

Twigs and Buds

Like a branch, a twig's job is to support and transport. Twigs support the leaves which have the important job of making food. Leaves need to collect the Sun's rays to make food so they must be held up as high as possible. Twigs also transport water *to* the leaves and sugars *from* the leaves, using tiny tubes.

Tale of a Twig

Choose a twig on your tree and find out its history: look at the **girdle scars** to find out how old it is; peel off the bud scales (the protective layer around the bud), and you will find a series of rings beneath. Each year a new bud grows. When the bud scales fall off a new girdle scar is left. Count the scars and you will know how old your twig is.

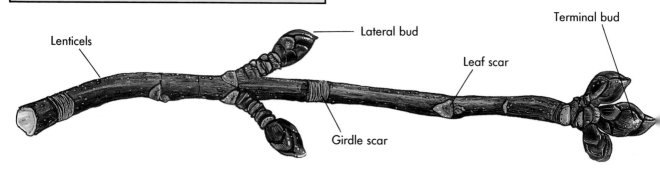

Lenticels

Lateral bud

Terminal bud

Leaf scar

Girdle scar

The shape at the end of the horse chestnut leaf is a horseshoe. Look on the twig for the **scar** left behind after the leaf fell. Can you see small dots in a semicircle in the scar? They are the holes where the **xylem** and **phloem** tubes are.

When the bud has opened, a new green twig is growing. Mark it with ballpoint pen at inch intervals. Measure these each day to see which part of your twig grows the most.

◀ This photograph shows the open bud scales with new twig and leaves emerging.

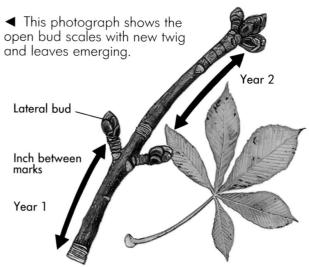

Year 2

Lateral bud

Inch between marks

Year 1

Where Do Buds Grow Best?

Pick three small twigs with buds that are about to open. Put them in pots of water. Leave one on a warm windowsill, leave the second in the refrigerator, and the third in a dark closet. Measure how much each twig grows each day. Compare the growth rates of your indoor twigs with a twig on your tree growing outside in the garden.

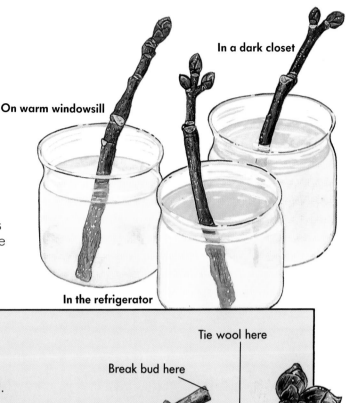

On warm windowsill

In a dark closet

In the refrigerator

Tag a Twig

New twigs and leaves come from the bud. See what happens when the main or **terminal** bud is knocked off. Tie some red wool around a twig growing on your tree and remove the terminal bud. Check every two days to see what happens.

Tie wool here

Break bud here

Buds and Leaves

Cut some buds in half to find out what is inside. Use large buds from different trees. Do they all look the same inside? Try opening the tiny leaves that are tucked inside. Look for tiny flowers too. Do all buds have scales on the outside? Bud scales protect the soft new leaves inside. The bud scales of the horse chestnut are sticky to protect them from hungry insects and birds.

Bud scales

Terminal bud

New Leaves

Look for new leaves that have just opened out from their bud. Use these pictures to help you work out how they were packed inside.

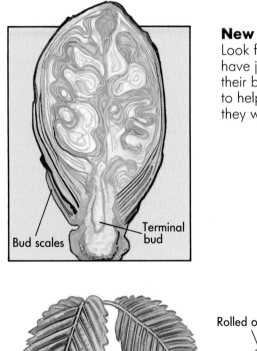

Curled up

Rolled over

Pleated

Folded up flat

13

Leaves

Try to imagine a world without leaves. All the trees and plants would be bare. Not only would the world look very dull (like a permanent winter scene) but humans and animals would have nothing to eat: leaves provide them with all their food because they turn sunlight into food energy. Leaves are also important as they make the oxygen in the air that we breathe.

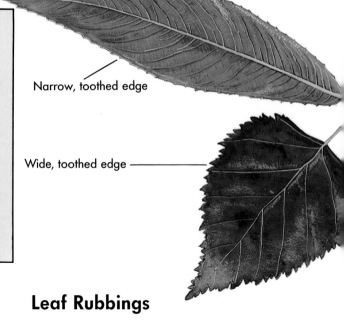

Narrow, toothed edge

Wide, toothed edge

Bags of Leaves

Collect leaves from as many different trees as you can find. Sort them into eight piles of leaves with different shapes. You will find that nearly all your leaves will be one of the eight kinds similar to the ones on these pages.

Leaf Painting

Choose some leaves with large veins or ribs. Paint the underside of the leaf with a thin layer of paint, then press the leaf carefully onto a clean, white sheet of paper. After a few seconds peel the leaf away. You will find that the shape of the leaf is painted onto the paper. Try this with different leaves.

Leaf Rubbings

Choose some leaves with large veins and ribs. Lay them upside down on a piece of paper. Lay another piece on top and hold it steady with one hand. Using the side of a wax crayon, rub evenly over the leaves. The shape of the leaf will gradually emerge. Compare these to your bark rubbings.

Painting Leaf Shadows

Hold your leaf firmly on a clean sheet of paper. Dip your brush well in the paint, and make brush strokes out onto the paper from the center of the leaf. When you have painted all around the leaf lift it off. A white shadow of your leaf remains. Make several leaf shadows on the same piece of paper and compare them. Make a collage of your leaf shadows.

Paint leaf

Press onto paper

Needles

Wide, large toothed edge

Wide, smooth edge

Narrow, smooth edge

Preserving Leaves

One way of preserving leaves is to press them for a few weeks between newspaper, under a heavy pile of books. Another way is to stand them for three weeks in a solution of glycerin and water. Add ⅔ hot water to ⅓ glycerin in a bucket. First crush and scrape the ends of the stems. The leaves turn brown and make good "everlasting" decorations.

Leaflets

Narrow, large toothed edge

A Family of Leaves

Collect lots of different leaves from the same tree. Make four piles from the smallest to the largest. Which is the most common size? Which part of the tree has big leaves and which part has smaller leaves? The leaves are different sizes because the smaller ones come from the shady areas which get less sunlight.

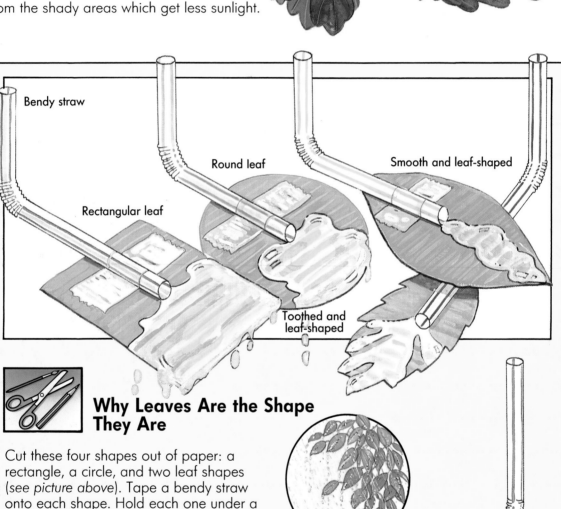

Bendy straw

Round leaf

Smooth and leaf-shaped

Rectangular leaf

Toothed and leaf-shaped

Why Leaves Are the Shape They Are

Cut these four shapes out of paper: a rectangle, a circle, and two leaf shapes (*see picture above*). Tape a bendy straw onto each shape. Hold each one under a faucet and allow water to drip slowly into the straw and notice what happens. Water collects on 1 and 2, until the structure gives way. If leaves were this shape they would be damaged by rain. Shapes 3 and 4 channel the water to the points and do not strain the leaf. They act as water drains. Do the same experiment with real leaves of different shapes and sizes.

Tree in the rain

Sun Traps and Food Producers

Leaves are like miniature food producers. They make food to help a plant or tree to survive. Humans and animals couldn't survive without these food producers either, because they live by eating them. Leaves use the Sun's energy, water, and carbon dioxide in the air to make food (sugars). They act like solar panels to trap the Sun's energy. You can see how much light they trap by holding up a sheet of white paper toward the Sun while standing near the tree's trunk. The surface will be dappled or completely covered by leaf shadows. The surface area of leaves traps nearly all the Sun's light.

▼ Looking up into a tree from underneath. Little of the sky is visible. This is because the leaves trap as much of the sunlight (energy) as they can to make food.

Sun

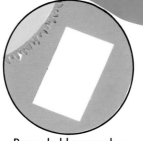

Sunlight + Water + Carbon dioxide

⇔

Sugars + Oxygen

Paper held near edge   Paper held near trunk

How Big Are Your Solar Panels?

Find the surface area of one leaf by drawing on a half-inch-square grid. Put your leaf on the grid and draw around it. Estimate the area by counting 1 for each square half covered or more and 0 for each square less than half covered.

To find the total area of our tree's solar panels we estimated the number of leaves on a small twig, the number of small twigs on a small branch, the number of small branches on a large branch, and the number of large branches on the trunk. Then we added it up.

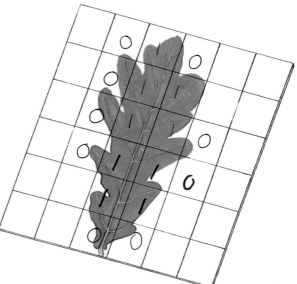

Why Trees lose Their Leaves

Leaves get worn and damaged and need to be replaced. On this page you will find out that some trees lose all their leaves at the same time, in the fall, and new leaves grow all at the same time, in spring. This kind are called **deciduous** trees. Other trees replace their leaves gradually throughout the year. They are called **evergreen** (because they always look green).

Which Side of the Leaf?

Leaves have holes in them called **stomata**. The tree loses water or **transpires** through these holes. Use two large leaves. Put Vaseline on the upper side of one and the under side of the other. Vaseline will fill up the holes. Cover each leaf with a small clear plastic bag. Secure around the leaf to make it airtight. Check your leaves every hour, especially if it is sunny weather. You will notice that more water is given off by the underside of the leaf. This is because it has more stomata than the upper side.

Losing Water

Trees lose water through leaves. You can prove this by picking two twigs of about the same size. Take the leaves off one twig, then put the twigs in separate pots with the *same* amount of water. Mark the water line on both pots. Put a small plastic bag around one set of leaves. Leave for a week. Check the water level every day. Notice in which pot the water goes down.

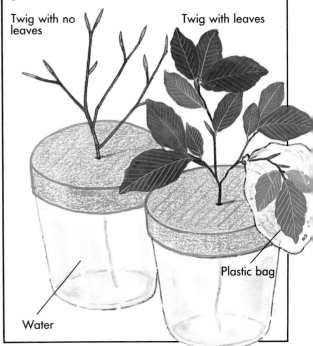

Twig with no leaves

Twig with leaves

Plastic bag

Water

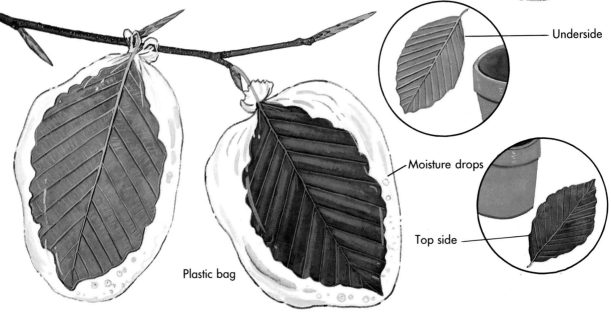

Plastic bag

Underside

Moisture drops

Top side

Deciduous and Evergreen

Trees cannot take in water through their roots in cold wintry weather. This means they would dry up or **dehydrate** if they didn't drop their leaves before winter. (Remember trees lose water — transpire — through their leaves.) Their leaves fall in the fall in preparation for the cold winter weather. But evergreens do not lose their leaves in the fall. So how is it that they don't dehydrate?

▶ Conifers have bendy branches and needlelike leaves so that snow can slip off and will not break the branches.

Investigating Evergreens

Collect a variety of evergreen leaves, holly, ivy, firs, spruce, cedar. Try the plastic bag experiment on these leaves and see what happens. Notice the hard waxy layer covering the leaf. This stops the leaf losing so much water.

Compare these with new deciduous leaves that are soft and fresh. Deciduous leaves lose water quickly and have a much greater surface area over which to lose water.

Holly

Scotch pine

Spruce

Different evergreen leaves

Imitating Winter

Pick a small twig of leaves. Put it in the freezer for an hour and then leave it in water for a few days and see what happens? Your leaves will be tricked into thinking winter is on the way. The deciduous ones should shrivel and fall. The shorter hours of daylight in the fall are also an important sign to trees that winter is on the way.

What Happens to a Leaf in the Fall?

Collect a bag of fall leaves and find out how they are changing color. Are they changing all over from green to yellow to brown? Elm leaves do this. Do the veins change color first or last, or does your leaf change color irregularly in blotches? By looking at your tree find out if the largest or the smallest leaves change color first.

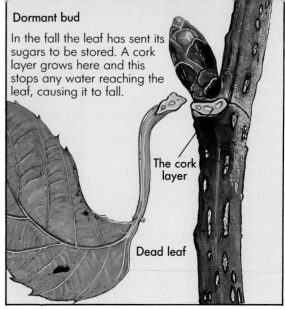

Dormant bud

In the fall the leaf has sent its sugars to be stored. A cork layer grows here and this stops any water reaching the leaf, causing it to fall.

The cork layer

Dead leaf

Color changes around veins first

Color changes between veins first

Color changes in irregular blotches

Why Leaves Change Color

Leaves have a yellow **pigment** (coloring) in them (some have red or orange pigments too). The green color of **chlorophyll** covers up these colors. In the fall the chlorophyll drains away. The yellow and red colors are left behind.

Leaf Skeleton

Find some large leaves with clear veins and ribs. Simmer the leaves at a low heat for half an hour in plenty of water. Leave them outside in a bucket for a few weeks. Now rinse your leaves in clean water to remove the decaying "flesh." Dabbing them with a soft paint brush will help. You will be left with the veins of your leaf. This is called a leaf skeleton. Stick your leaf skeletons on cardboard to make attractive greeting cards or bookmarks.

Cross a Leaf

Put some colored or masking tape on a green leaf in the shape of a cross. Leave the leaf on the tree. If leaves can't get light they cannot make chlorophyll. After a few days you should be able to see the yellow pigment showing under the tape.

Tape over leaf

Veins

Leaf Pictures

Collect your favorite leaves. Look for special colors and shapes. Lay them flat between several sheets of newspaper and leave them under a heavy object. After about a week your leaves should be dried and pressed. You can display them by sticking them on your windows (use a dab of glue). You can also make pictures by glueing them down. Try making trees, flowers, figures, and abstract patterns. Pressed colored leaves make good cards and bookmarks. Mount them on a sheet of cardboard and cover them with sticky-backed plastic.

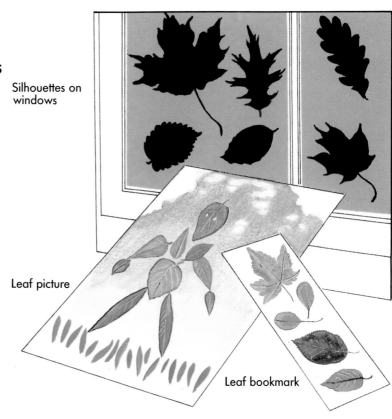

Silhouettes on windows

Leaf picture

Leaf bookmark

What Happens to Leaves?

When leaves fall in a wood they form a thick crunchy carpet. If trees drop a layer of leaves 8 inches deep each year, after 10 years there would be more than a 6-foot thick carpet of them! This doesn't happen because leaves are made of organic material (this means they were once living). When organic things die they **decompose** or rot. Put 10 leaves in a tin, leave them for four weeks, and check regularly to see what happens. Find out if all leaves decompose at the same rate: pin down various leaves under plastic netting.

Rotting leaves

Leaves under net

Where Do Trees Come From?

Animals start life as a tiny egg. Plants begin life as a small seed such as an acorn. Seeds hold all the "growing information" for a new tree to develop but need certain conditions to **germinate** or begin growing. Once it has started growing and has its own leaves it can then use the Sun's energy to make its own food.

▲ An oak tree seedling growing out of an acorn. The root begins to grow first. This splits open the shell of the acorn. The shoot then begins to grow, using the food stored in the acorn halves.

Sorting Tree Seeds

Different trees produce different kinds of seeds. Some produce seeds in a fleshy covering — a fruit or berry; some produce seeds tucked into the folds of cones or catkins; some produce seeds with wings and others produce seeds inside nuts or pods.

Go for a walk and see how many seeds from trees you can find. Sort them into these six categories (kinds). Look for seeds from trees in the kitchen too (nuts and fruits).

Fruits **Cones** **Catkins**

Seeds with Wings **Pods** **Nuts**

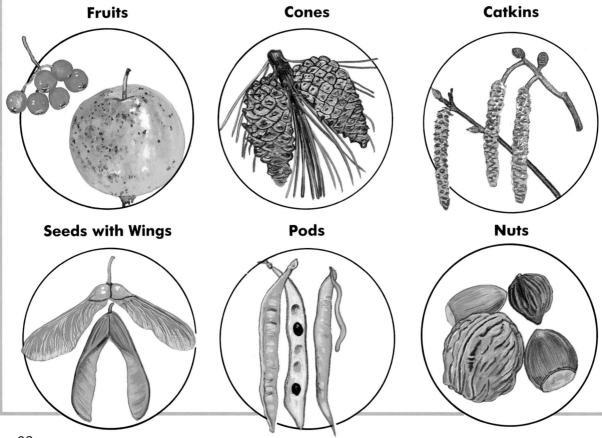

Tree Fruits In the Kitchen

Many of the fruits we eat such as apples, bananas, and pears come from trees. A fruit is a fleshy wrapping for a seed. Cut up some of your kitchen fruits and see if you can find the seeds inside. Tomatoes and cucumbers are fruits too: they have seeds with a fleshy case around them. Try growing some trees from fruit seeds: orange, apple, and pear seeds will sometimes grow. Start them off by putting them on a saucer with damp cotton balls.

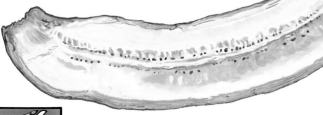

Apple

Pear

Banana

Growing Wild Trees

Try growing some wild seeds and fruits, such as acorns, elderberries, hawthorns, and hazelnut which are easy to find. Make up, or buy, a tray of potting compost. Make rows in the compost about half an inch deep with the end of a pencil. Sprinkle about 50 of the smaller seeds along these rows. Make holes an inch deep for the medium-sized berries, and an inch and a half deep for the large seeds and cover them with soil. Put them in a warm sunny position and keep the compost moist. Do not be disappointed if they don't germinate. Some seeds lie **dormant** for many years.

Walking Seeds

Plants cannot walk. Trees and other plants make tasty fruits around their seeds in order to tempt animals to eat them. In this way the seeds can be carried all over the world inside an animal's gut. The fleshy part is digested, but the hard case around the seed will be left in the animal's dropping.

Elder flower

Elder berry

Elder tree

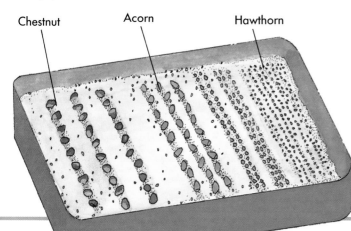

Chestnut

Acorn

Hawthorn

Estimating Elder Seeds

Count how many seeds there are in one elderberry by squashing it. Count how many berries there are in the cluster. Estimate how many clusters of berries are on the tree. You can now estimate how many seeds there are altogether.

How Do Other Trees Travel?

Animals such as squirrels store nuts and often forget where they have put them, and these later grow into trees. In the fall when there is plenty of wild food about, badgers and foxes will often eat fruits and berries as an alternative to meat. The pips and seeds will be discarded in their droppings. These may grow into new trees a long way from the parent tree and this is called dispersal.

Squirrel storing nuts

Barometer Cones

Collect some cones from different **conifers**. Larch, pine, or spruce are good. Put some in a dry, warm place and others in a damp place. Leave them for several days and see what happens. Cones have moisture sensitive cells at their center. These cause the folds of the cone to open when the weather is dry and close when it is damp.

Catkins and Pods

Birch seeds hang down from the tree, tucked in the folds of a catkin. When the seeds are ripe, the folds of the catkin open and the wind blows them out. Laburnum, locust, and Judas trees produce seeds in pods. On a very hot dry day the pods burst open. They twist, causing the seeds to be thrown out in different directions.
Warning: laburnum seeds are very poisonous.

Crossbills

Crossbills are the only birds that can extract the seeds from a closed cone. This means that there is always plenty of food for them to eat. A nest of young crossbills can eat over 85,000 pine seeds as they grow up. The parents twist the cones off the stem then prise open the cones using their specially designed beak. Try extracting a seed using a pair of tweezers.

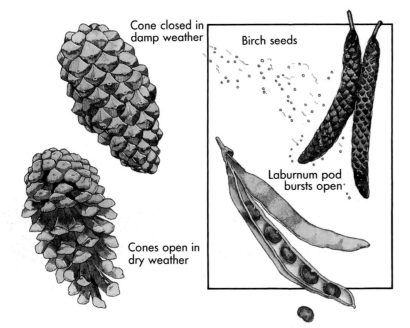

Cone closed in damp weather

Birch seeds

Laburnum pod bursts open

Cones open in dry weather

Crossbill

Flying Seeds Game

Make a tree and base as shown. Make 20 seeds out of small rectangles of paper: twist them in the middle. Balance the seeds in the tree. To play the game, blow gently on your tree. If your seed lands in the flower bed or on the lawn it will be picked up by a careful gardener (remove these ones). Seeds landing on concrete or in the pond will not germinate. If the seed lands in the wild garden, it can germinate. To find out if it germinates you must throw a die.

- If you throw a 1, your seedling is killed by weedkiller.
- Throw a 2, seedling killed by drought.
- Throw a 3, weather is warm, wet, and sunny. Seedling survives.
- Throw a 4, frosts kill your seedling.
- Throw a 5, seedling is cared for and watered by a child. It survives.
- Throw a 6, squirrel eats seedling.

Play the game five times (100 seeds in total). How many grow into new trees?

Equipment: paper, paint, glue.

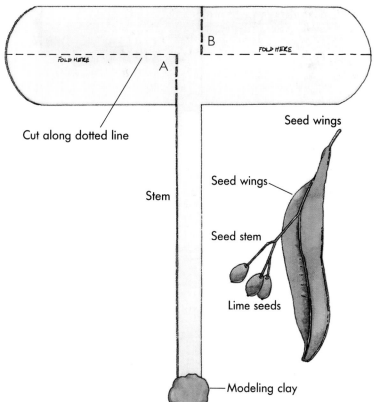

Balance seeds on the branches

Lawn

Flower bed

Pond

Wild Garden

Concrete

Helicopter Seeds

Some seeds, such as sycamore are formed so that as they drop they start to spin like the blades of a helicopter.

Make your own lime "helicopter" by cutting a shape like this in thin cardboard. Cut along the dotted lines. Stick a small blob of modeling clay on the bottom. This provides the weight of the seed. Fold the "blades" of the helicopter up at point (A) and down at point (B). You may need to experiment with the angle to get your seed to fly properly.

FOLD HERE

B

FOLD HERE

A

Cut along dotted line

Stem

Seed wings

Seed wings

Seed stem

Lime seeds

Modeling clay

Where Seeds Come From

If you look at some trees you can see the seeds developing at different stages from the ovary of the flower to the fully grown fruit or seed.

Look at sycamore, cherry, elder, and apple trees when they are flowering and notice the tiny fruits beginning to grow where the petals have fallen off. A good way to watch the growth of a flower into a seed is to tie a bright piece of wool around the stem of the flower so you always know which one to look at. Return ever few days to see what has happened. Remember not all ova are fertilized and grow into seeds.

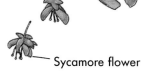

Sycamore flower

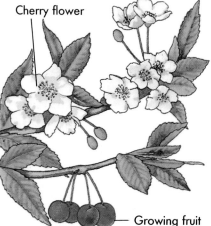

Cherry flower

Growing fruit

Male and Female

Look closely into some flowers on a tree. Look for the **stamens** with **pollen** (the male part) and the **ovary** (the female part). This picture shows you what they look like. Pollen from one flower must be transferred to the ovary of another flower, then it can grow into a fruit or seed.

Be a "Feather Bee"

You can help to make fruit trees grow more fruit by pollinating the flowers. Using a feather or your finger, pick up pollen from one flower and then dust it onto another flower. This takes the male pollen to the female part. They grow together to make a seed. Fruit growers spray their trees with insecticides. It is important that this does not harm the bees. They fly to the flower looking for nectar (food). They also collect pollen to feed their young. Some of this pollen is brushed off onto other flowers.

This photograph shows bees collecting nectar and pollen on fruit flowers.

Cooking with Fruits

Wash eight elderberry clusters and remove the berries. Core and slice four apples and one orange with its peel on. Simmer all the fruit for half an hour. If necessary, add sugar. Transfer to an oven-proof dish, make a pastry top, and cook for half an hour at 350°F until lightly brown.

A pleasant summer drink can be made from elderflowers. Pick 15 heads and remove the stalks, which taste bitter. Pour in a pint of boiling water. Add the juice and rind of two lemons and 3 ounces of sugar. Strain and serve.

Fruit Printing

Moist, firm fruits are good to use as "printing blocks." Apples, strawberries, and pears work well. Mix up some paints in flat containers. Cut the fruit in half and dip it into the paint. Press the fruit gently onto a clean piece of paper and lift.

Help a Hazel

In some trees the male and female parts are separate. The hazel tree has small red flowers. Look for them in this picture. The male pollen is produced on catkins that hang down from the branches. The flowers are so small that insects like the bee do not bother to visit them. You can "help a hazel" by taking pollen from the catkins to the flower. You imitate the wind by gently shaking the twig. If the pollen is ripe, it falls easily. Willow, poplar, birch, alder, and oak also have hanging catkins carrying the male pollen. They all need the wind to help them pollinate the female flowers.

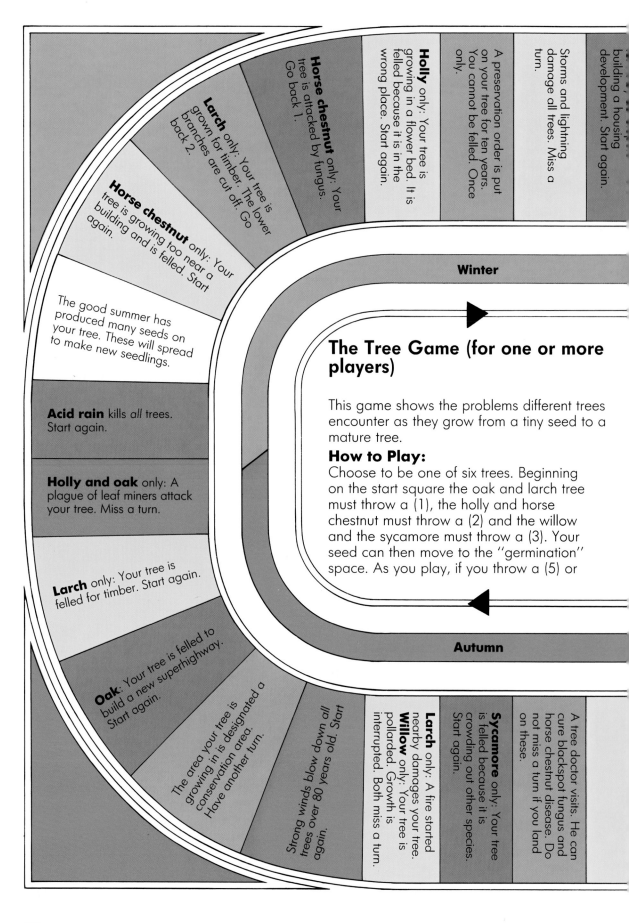

The Tree Game (for one or more players)

This game shows the problems different trees encounter as they grow from a tiny seed to a mature tree.

How to Play:

Choose to be one of six trees. Beginning on the start square the oak and larch tree must throw a (1), the holly and horse chestnut must throw a (2) and the willow and the sycamore must throw a (3). Your seed can then move to the "germination" space. As you play, if you throw a (5) or

Winter

...building a housing development. Start again.

Storms and lightning damage all trees. Miss a turn.

A preservation order is put on your tree for ten years. You cannot be felled. Once only.

Holly only: Your tree is growing in a flower bed. It is felled because it is in the wrong place. Start again.

Horse chestnut only: Your tree is attacked by fungus. Go back 1.

Larch only: Your tree is grown for timber. The lower branches are cut off. Go back 2.

Horse chestnut only: Your tree is growing too near a building and is felled. Start again.

The good summer has produced many seeds on your tree. These will spread to make new seedlings.

Acid rain kills *all* trees. Start again.

Holly and oak only: A plague of leaf miners attack your tree. Miss a turn.

Larch only: Your tree is felled for timber. Start again.

Oak: Your tree is felled to build a new superhighway. Start again.

The area your tree is growing in is designated a conservation area. Have another turn.

Strong winds blow all trees over 80 years old down. Start again.

Autumn

Larch only: A fire started nearby damages your tree. Your tree is felled because it is crowding out other species. Start again.

Willow only: Your tree is pollarded. Growth is interrupted. Both miss a turn.

Sycamore only: Your tree is felled because it is crowding out other species. Start again.

A tree doctor visits. He can cure blackspot fungus and horse chestnut disease. Do not miss a turn if you land on these.

28

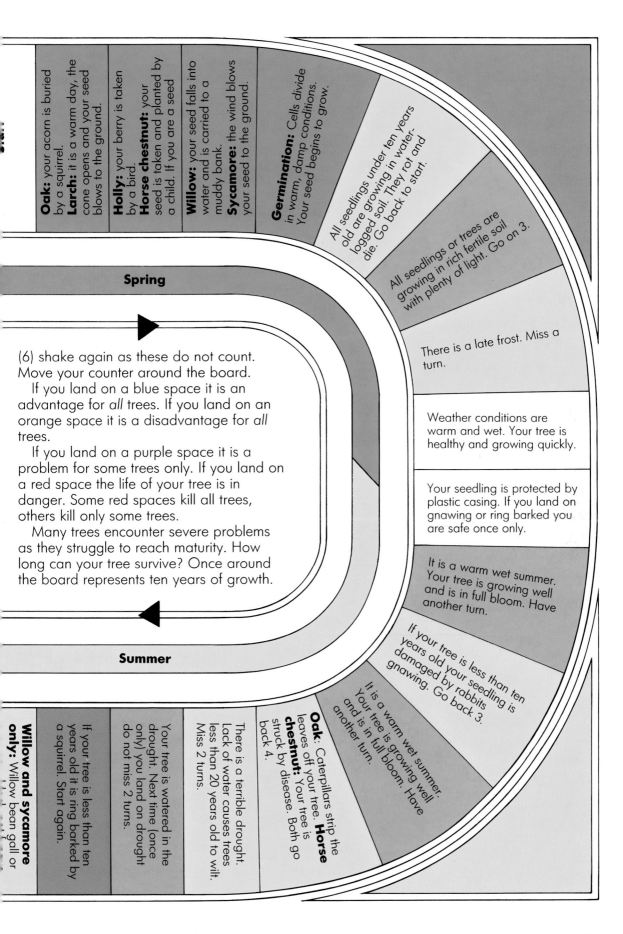

Oak: your acorn is buried by a squirrel.

Larch: it is a warm day, the cone opens and your seed blows to the ground.

Holly: your berry is taken by a bird.

Horse chestnut: your seed is taken and planted by a child. If you are a seed

Willow: your seed falls into water and is carried to a muddy bank.

Sycamore: the wind blows your seed to the ground.

Germination: Cells divide in warm, damp conditions. Your seed begins to grow.

All seedlings under ten years old are growing in water-logged soil. They rot and die. Go back to start.

All seedlings or trees are growing in rich fertile soil with plenty of light. Go on 3.

There is a late frost. Miss a turn.

Weather conditions are warm and wet. Your tree is healthy and growing quickly.

Your seedling is protected by plastic casing. If you land on gnawing or ring barked you are safe once only.

It is a warm wet summer. Your tree is growing well and is in full bloom. Have another turn.

If your tree is less than ten years old your seedling is damaged by rabbits gnawing. Go back 3.

It is a warm wet summer. Your tree is growing well and is in full bloom. Have another turn.

Oak: Caterpillars strip the leaves off your tree. **Horse chestnut:** Your tree is struck by disease. Both go back 4.

There is a terrible drought. Lack of water causes trees less than 20 years old to wilt. Miss 2 turns.

Your tree is watered in the drought. Next time (once only) you land on drought do not miss 2 turns.

If your tree is less than ten years old it is ring barked by a squirrel. Start again.

Willow and sycamore only: Willow bean gall or

Spring

Summer

(6) shake again as these do not count. Move your counter around the board.

If you land on a blue space it is an advantage for *all* trees. If you land on an orange space it is a disadvantage for *all* trees.

If you land on a purple space it is a problem for some trees only. If you land on a red space the life of your tree is in danger. Some red spaces kill all trees, others kill only some trees.

Many trees encounter severe problems as they struggle to reach maturity. How long can your tree survive? Once around the board represents ten years of growth.

The World of a Tree

Every tree is a world of its own. It is home for thousands of different plants and creatures. We have found over 100 different species of animal and plant living in or using our oak. Up to 250 species of insect like living on oak trees.

Creatures and plants are **dependent** on each other in different ways. Many mammals, birds, and insects are dependent on trees and plants as a source of food and shelter. Some creatures and trees are mutually dependent: they both need each other to survive. For example, this tree provides food for minibeasts and small mammals, and they help to convert the tree's decaying leaves into rich soil.

▼ Spotted Woodpecker

Squirrel Drey
Squirrels build two kinds of dreys. This is a winter drey. In summer they build dreys for rearing their young in the branches away from the trunk.

Plants and Flowers
Some plants such as the bluebell flourish under trees in spring before the leaves come out.

Leaf Litter
Dead leaves collect and rot under a tree. They make a marvelous home for minibeasts.

Nests

Small birds nest in small trees. Larger birds nest in high open branches.

Other Things to Look For

Some things are harmful to trees. Ivy can grow as high as the tree itself. This weakens the tree by reducing the light supply to the leaves and prevents them photosynthesising. Fungi grow on both dead and living trees. Bracket fungi are known to kill many trees every year.

Some insects are harmful to trees. The elm bark beetle has caused the death of millions of trees in Europe. The beetle carries a fungus that kills the tree. You may notice some of the leaves on your tree have pale wiggly lines or blotches on them. These are the secret passages made by leaf-mining grubs which tunnel, eating between the different layers of a leaf and later turn into moths. Another word for a tree's community is its **ecosystem.**

Algae and Lichens

Algae are minute single-cell plants that often grow on tree trunks. They look like a fine green powder. Lichens can be green, gray, yellow, or orange.

Fox Home

Foxes often dig their dens among the roots of trees where they can rear up to five young cubs every year.

Deer Browsing

Deer and cattle often eat leaves off the lower branches of trees. In the fall deer will also eat acorns and beech mast.

Who Lives in Your Tree?

You can find out who lives in your tree by shaking the branches and catching the creatures as they fall out. Get two friends to hold a white sheet out under the branch while you shake. Try using stiff white paper if you have no one to help you.

The Blue Carpet

In spring, under the trees in some woods, the ground looks blue. Bluebells thrive by growing in spring when there are few leaves on the trees and plenty of light can filter through. Plants need light to survive and grow. Can anything grow under a tree in summer when there is a dense covering of leaves? Check what grows at different times of the year.

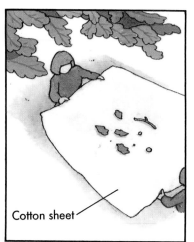

Cotton sheet

Hawthorn leaf gall

Robin's pincushion gall

Oak cherry gall

Oak spangle gall

Plant galls are abnormal swellings on the leaves of plants. They are the result of attack by fungi or insects, mites, or even small worms. The largest are caused by insects which lay their eggs in the tissue of the leaf. When the larvae grow up they cause huge swelling of the leaf.

Looking in Leaf Litter

When dead leaves collect under a tree, they form what is known as **leaf litter**. Find out what lives in the leaf litter or soil beneath your tree. Here are some of the creatures you might find. They help to decompose the leaves and twigs that fall off your tree. Collect some in a tub and see how they behave.

▼ A carpet of bluebells.

Actual size —

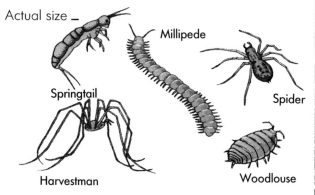

Millipede

Springtail

Spider

Harvestman

Woodlouse

Mammal Signs

It is difficult to see wild animals in their natural habitat (home). This is because they are wary of humans, and because many are nocturnal. Even if we can't see animals such as foxes, badgers, and rabbits, there are often plenty of clues to look for. Footprints tell us which animals are about, where they came from and where they went to. Droppings tell us what the animal ate during a recent meal.

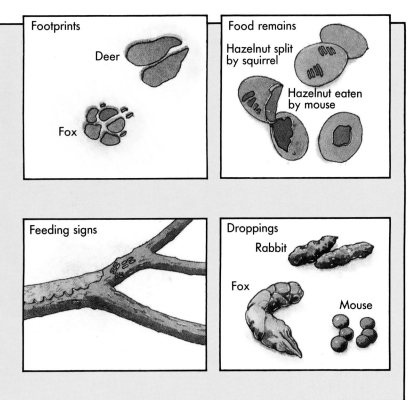

Footprints

Deer

Fox

Food remains

Hazelnut split by squirrel

Hazelnut eaten by mouse

Feeding signs

Droppings

Rabbit

Fox

Mouse

Bird Signs

Look for feathers, droppings, and pellets to see which birds visit the tree. A pile of droppings all in one place usually means a bird has been roosting there. Look for the short downy "body" feathers and the longer wing and tail feathers. Owl pellets are a mass of fur and bones that the owl cannot digest. They are coughed up again as a pellet.

More Plants on Trees

Look for mosses growing on and under your tree. Make a miniature moss garden where tiny creatures might like to live, using small flowers and stones. Mistletoe is a **parasite** (something that lives and feeds off another living thing). Birds wipe the seeds from their beaks onto the tree. Roots then grow into the wood and suck up the **sap**.

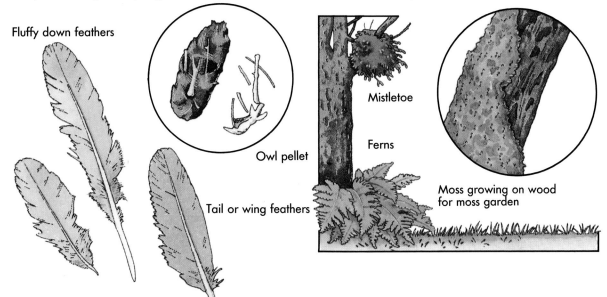

Fluffy down feathers

Owl pellet

Tail or wing feathers

Mistletoe

Ferns

Moss growing on wood for moss garden

The Importance of Wood

Wood has been used by humans for thousands of years. It was first fashioned into simple tools and burned to produce heat. Wood has been used to build houses, bridges, ships, and furniture. Wood is used to make paper, so without trees the printing revolution could never have taken place.

▲ Wood is used for many purposes. Many of the objects in this picture are made of wood.

A World Without Wood

How many things can you find in the photograph on this page that are made of wood? There are a great many if you look closely enough. Now try noting down all the things in your house that are made of wood. You will find that a great many things in your house rely on wood for their basic structure or support.

A World Without Trees

Every time you switch on a light, energy is being used. That energy originally came from trees and is now in its turn causing the death of other trees. Much of the electricity we use today is generated by burning coal (made from dead plants and trees). When coal is burned, acid gases are released and collect high up in the atmosphere. Here they mix with water to form **acid rain**. Acid rain has terrible effects on the environment. It pollutes rivers and lakes, killing fish and plants; it eats into stone and destroys the surface of buildings; it helps to poison the soil and damages trees, eventually killing them. About 15 per cent of forests in Europe have been destroyed already. Acid rain can be as strong as vinegar.

Cars of the Future

Cars are also big polluters. They give off huge amounts of pollutant gases. Cars have been developed with special devices to make exhaust gases harmless. The Brazilians have come up with an interesting alternative: they run cars on alcohol made from sugar cane, which, if successful, will save much of the Earth's resources.

Trees damaged by acid rain.

Car exhausts cause acid rain.

Making Paper from Paper

To make your own paper, wash a large newspaper. Tear (or liquidise) it into shreds, put it into a bucket and pour in hot water. Allow to soak overnight. Boil this mixture in a large old saucepan until the paper has dissolved into a mushy stew. Let it stand and cool so that there is an even layer floating near the surface. Dip the mesh into the pan and lift it out flat so that the pulp makes a layer of even thickness. Let the water drain away, then turn the paper out onto a piece of old blanket. Add a few layers so that the paper will hold together. Place another piece of old blanket on top and then a wooden board. Tread on the board to squeeze out all the water. Lift the blanket off, and leave to dry. If the mesh is too floppy, pin it to a wooden frame.

Did you know? Big paper mills can make over 20 miles of paper per hour working day and night. That is 480 miles a day!

Equipment: Newspaper, fine plastic mesh, bucket, saucepan, old blanket.

Plenty of Paper

Paper is important as a way of recording and passing on information. We use it for newspapers, books, maps, letters, and many other forms of writing. Paper can also be used for other things: tissues, paper towels, bags, and packages. Look around your home, you will find many different uses for paper.

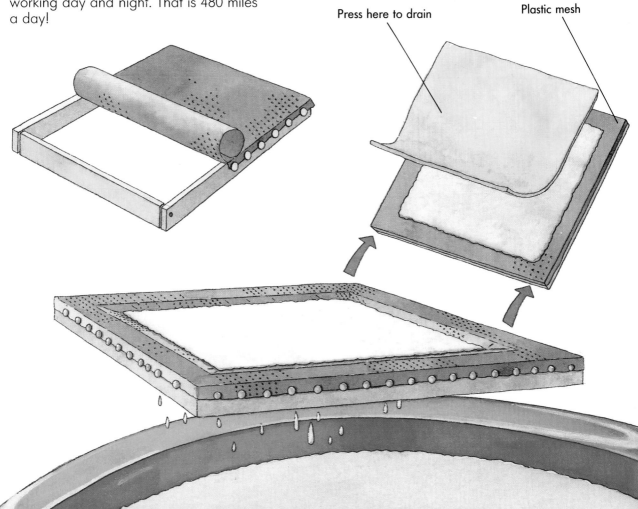

Press here to drain

Plastic mesh

Using Wood

It is very important that the woods that now survive do so for many years to come. Woods survive best if they are properly looked after and one way of helping is making sure that the trees are not overcrowded. Cutting some down actually helps the others to grow better and provides valuable wood for building and heating, and paper-making.

Managing Woodland

People look after woodland to make it grow the way they want it to. Hazel trees are coppiced: they are cut back to ground level to allow new straight stems to grow up. These are used as poles or for fencing. Willow trees are pollarded: the branches are cut back at a higher level and the willow "wands" are harvested for basket weaving.

Coppiced at ground level

Pollarded at 10–13 feet

Making a Garden Broom

Get an adult to help you make this. Cut a yard length of ash, lime or hazel wood to use as the handle. Use birch twigs for the head. Drill an inch hole through the handle. Fit a peg tightly into this hole. Hold a bundle of twigs around the handle and bind them tightly, then fasten the cord carefully to the peg. These brooms are excellent for sweeping up autumn leaves.

Equipment: Wooden pole, birch twigs, cord.

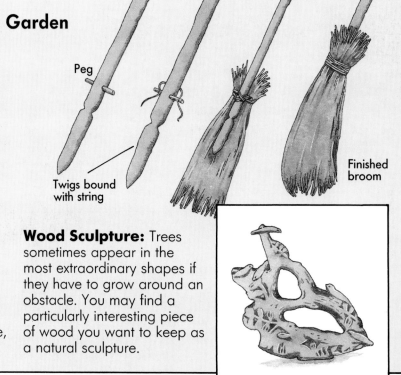

Peg

Twigs bound with string

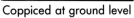

Finished broom

Wood Sculpture: Trees sometimes appear in the most extraordinary shapes if they have to grow around an obstacle. You may find a particularly interesting piece of wood you want to keep as a natural sculpture.

Building a Bird Box

You will need a plank of wood about 6 inches wide, half an inch thick and 5 feet long. Mark on the measurements of each part before beginning to cut your wood. Saw up the six pieces and sand the edges smooth. Drill a hole about an inch in diameter in the front of your box. If you make the hole a little larger (up to 1¼ inches) you will attract different kinds of bird to nest there. Assemble your box by joining it together as shown. Use screws or galvanized nails. Fasten the lid with a catch to stop cats interfering.

Equipment: Plank of wood, drill, screws.

Size of Hole

Make sure the size of the hole is the same as shown here. The box is designed only for quite small birds and if the hole is too big they will be forced out by stronger species.

You can attract different types of bird by making a more open box. Saw off the upper half of the front by sawing along the dotted lines as shown.

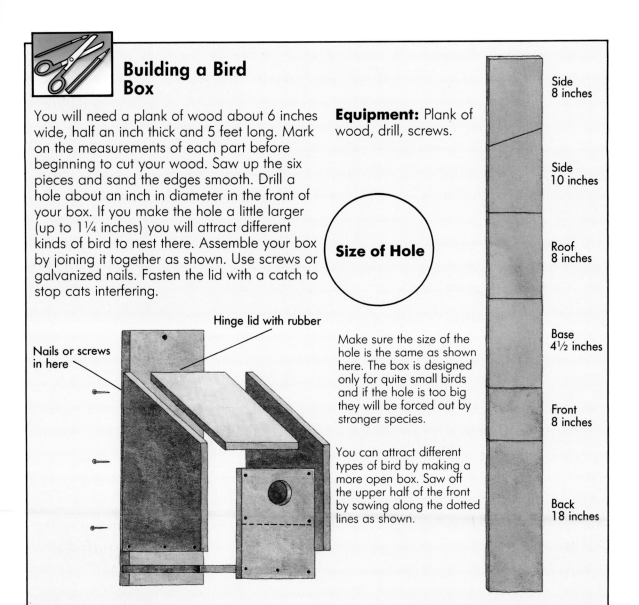

Nails or screws in here

Hinge lid with rubber

Side 8 inches

Side 10 inches

Roof 8 inches

Base 4½ inches

Front 8 inches

Back 18 inches

Where to Put It

Hang or nail your box to a tree about 10 to 15 feet off the ground and safely out of reach of any cats. Do not let it face into strong sunlight as this can kill nestlings. Facing northeast or southeast is preferable. Remember to clean the box every fall so that old nest material doesn't collect inside. If you do not, the box will become clogged up and new birds will not come and nest inside.

Remember to hang the box out of reach of any cats.

Remember to hang your box in the shade.

Disappearing Forests

Many thousands of years ago three-fourths of all land was covered by trees. Through disease, fire and felling between 70 and 90 percent has been destroyed. Some countries still have large areas of rain forest but these are rapidly being destroyed.

▲ Rain forests are cut down to provide grazing land and places for people to live. Often these ventures fail but the forest is terminally damaged.

The Rich Rain Forest and How It Helps us

Rain forests are full of plants and animals, many of which are useful to us. Some 40 percent of medical chemicals in the United States come from rain forests. Many more chemicals are still undiscovered. Trees also produce a large amount of the oxygen that we breathe. This picture shows that leaves take in carbon dioxide (CO_2) that we breathe out, and give off oxygen (O_2). Imagine what would happen if all the trees and plants that make oxygen for us were destroyed. Every minute over 100 acres of forest are destroyed. Once the trees are gone the rich soil is washed away by heavy rains so no more trees can grow.

How You Can Help

We need wood, and it is not a bad thing to fell trees so long as they are replanted. You can help by planting trees in your garden or at school. You can often find self-sown tree seedlings near a well established tree that might not survive well in the shade. These could be moved to a more suitable open place. You can, of course, buy trees at a tree nursery.

You can help by recycling old newspaper. Some councils now have special collecting points. Find out by phoning your local council offices. Trees are destroyed by acid rain. Help prevent this by saving energy and recycling.

Many South American Indians live in the rain forest. They have a legend that tells how the trees hold up the sky and that if they are cut down a great catastrophe will come about.

Did you know? It takes one tree to make 250 disposable diapers. Can you estimate how many trees each baby needs in a year? Every minute an area of rain forest the size of 20 football fields is destroyed. How can we support the people who are trying to save it?

Acid Rain

Index

Editors: Thomas Keegan and Annabel Warburg
Designer: Ben White
Illustrators: David More ●
Liz Peperell

Cover Design: Terry Woodley
Picture Research: Elaine Willis

The authors would like to thank their colleagues from the South Oxfordshire Countryside Education Trust, especially Jackie Flynn, and the many others who have helped with ideas for this book.

The publishers wish to thank the following for supplying photographs for this book:

Page 8 Rosie Harlow; 12 NHPA/L.Campbell; 17 NHPA/S.Dalton; 19 ZEFA; 22 NHPA/S.Dalton; 26 NHPA/S.Dalton; 27 NHPA/B.Hawkes; 30 NHPA/S.Dalton; 31 Heather Angel/Biofotos; 32 Nature Photographers; 34 Rosie Harlow; 36 NHPA/E.A.Janes; 38 Nature Photographers; 39 Rosie Harlow.

Published in 1991 by Warwick Press, 387 Park Avenue South, New York, New York 10016
First published in 1991 by Kingfisher Books
© Grisewood & Dempsey Ltd. 1991

6 5 4 3 2 1
All rights reserved
Printed in Hong Kong

LIBRARY OF CONGRESS CATALOGING-IN-PUBLICATION DATA

Harlow, Rosie
  Trees and Leaves / Rosie Harlow and Gareth Morgan
    p.cm. – (Fun with science)
  Includes index.
  Summary: Simple experiments introduce various aspects of trees and leaves.
  ISBN 0–531–19126–5
  1. Trees—Juvenile literature. 2. Leaves—Juvenile literature. 3. Trees—Experiments—Juvenile literature. 4. Leaves—Experiments—Juvenile literature. 5. Forest conservation—Juvenile literature.
  [1. Trees—Experiments. 2. Leaves—Experiments. 3. Experiments.]

  I. Morgan, Gareth. II. Title. III. Series
QK475.8.M67   1991   91–7461
582.16—dc20   CIP
                         93-1099   AC